OHIO
DOMINICAN
UNIVERSITY™

SINCE 1911

Will Rogers

An American Legend

★

Written by
FRANK KEATING

Illustrated by
MIKE WIMMER

SILVER WHISTLE
HARCOURT, INC.

San Diego   New York   London

*The author and illustrator gratefully acknowledge the help of
the following people and organizations in the making of this
book:*

   The Will Rogers Museum, Claremore, Oklahoma
   Michelle Carter
   Joseph Carter
   The Will Rogers Memorial Commission, Claremore, Oklahoma

Library of Congress Cataloging-in-Publication Data
Keating, Frank, 1937–
Will Rogers: an American legend/Frank Keating; illustrated by
Mike Wimmer.
p. cm.
"Silver Whistle."
Summary: A biography of the man from Oklahoma, known for his
wise and witty sayings.
1. Rogers, Will, 1879–1935—Juvenile literature. 2. Entertainers—
United States—Biography—Juvenile literature. 3. Humorists,
American—20th century—Biography—Juvenile literature.
[1. Rogers, Will, 1879–1935. 2. Entertainers. 3. Humorists.
4. Cherokee Indians—Biography. 5. Indians of North America—
Biography.] I. Title.
PN2287.R74K39 2002
792.7'028'092—dc21   2001005949
ISBN 0-15-202405-0

First edition
H G F E D C B A

Printed in Singapore

The illustrations in this book were painted in oil on canvas.
The display type was set in Windsor Light.
The text type was set in Love Letter Typewriter.
Color separations by Bright Arts Ltd., Hong Kong
Printed and bound by Tien Wah Press, Singapore
This book was printed on totally chlorine-free Nymolla Matte Art paper.
Production supervision by Sandra Grebenar and Pascha Gerlinger
Designed by Ivan Holmes

BIBLIOGRAPHY

Carter, Joseph H. *Never Met a Man I Didn't Like: The Life and
Writings of Will Rogers.* New York: Avon Books, 1991.

Rogers, Will. *Wise and Witty Sayings of a Great American
Humorist.* Compiled by Art Wortman. [Kansas City, Mo.]:
Hallmark Editions, 1969.

To those brave and courageous citizens of Oklahoma,
who showed our state to be so special after
April 19, 1995.

                                              --F. K.

To the land and people of Oklahoma, a place where
the soil yields a bountiful yield, in good crops and
better people. A place that I am proud to call Home.

                                              --M. W.

WILL ROGERS stood in the center of the stage,

twirling a lariat.

One day he would travel the world as few men had

and return to say,

"I never met a man I didn't like."

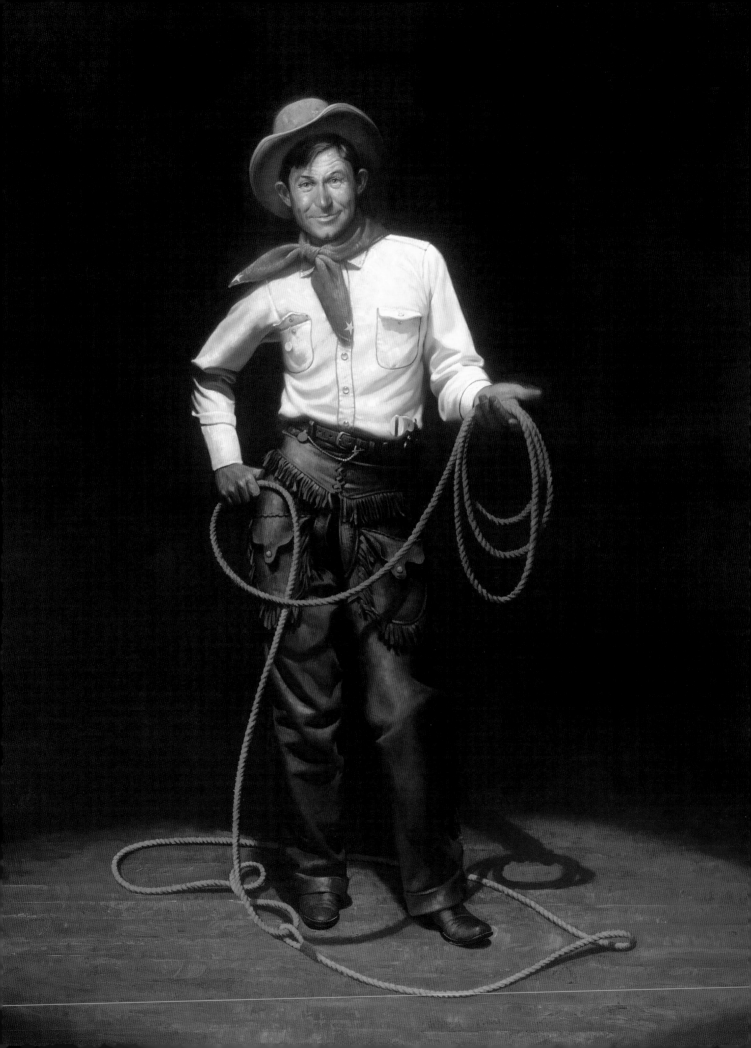

Will as a boy was called to adventure.

The youngest of eight children, he was born in 1879

in Indian Territory.

There, on the broad back of his father's horse, Lummox,

and at his mother's knee, he saw oceans of wheat

and dreamed of touching distant skies. And he

began to read.

"To learn is to read," Will Rogers said.

Will Rogers was an Oklahoma boy,

raised on a ranch, part Cherokee Indian.

A member of the Paint Clan,

he learned to ride and rope as well as any boy or man.

Riding and roping, they said of Will, so that one day

he could "lasso the tail off a blowfly."

Will raced across the prairie on his horse Comanche,
lassoing goats and wild turkeys.
For practice. For adventure.
That was what boys did in those days,
before farmers and barbed wire fence.
"A man that don't love a horse, there is something
the matter with him," Will Rogers believed.

Will's lot in life was ten years or so in school.

But travel, and reading, and poking and probing,

those were Will's lifetime school.

"A man only learns by two things," Will Rogers said.

"One is reading, and the other is association with

smarter people."

Will Rogers loved the land,

from the sparkling waters of the Verdigris River

to the Oklahoma hills.

The land taught him that all men were good,

that each had something to say,

and that humility and honesty came from a rural life.

"No man is great if he thinks he is," Will Rogers said.

Will flew everywhere he could. Always restless.

Everyone he met became his friend.

Everyplace he visited broadened his mind.

He was always joking and sharing with others

the humor and joy of living.

"I can't tell you where to write," he said, "for I don't

know where I will be..."

Will always seemed to be in motion.

Two dozen coast-to-coast flights across the United States,

flights into Russia and across southeast Asia.

Three trips around the world when flight was new.

Driven and impatient to go and see more, he said,

"If your time is worth anything, travel by air.

If not, you might just as well walk."

Will quickly returned from his travels to his family.

To Betty and to their four children:

Will Jr., Mary, Jimmy, and Fred.

They went to California, where Will built a corral

on the lot of a movie studio.

He roped. And he played with Betty and their children.

"I am just an old country boy in a big town

trying to get along."

Will was known far and wide.

When times were bad, Will Rogers made people hope.

When times were good, he made people laugh.

He spoke common sense to common people.

He spoke to the "old common fellow,"

to lift him up, to make a child smile,

and to give all the courage to go on.

Will poked fun at the big and the not-so-big.

To make a point. To say something true.

"You can always joke good naturedly with a big man.

That's why he's big!" Will said.

Across the nation, families laughed with him on

radio broadcasts, in newspaper columns, and in movies.

"All I know is what I read in the papers," he said.

Will wrote as he spoke:

simple, true, thoughtful, and wise.

Life by laughter.

Common sense from an uncommon common man.

"They may call me a rube and a hick, but I would
rather be the man who bought the Brooklyn Bridge
than the man who sold it."

Will taught modesty and plain living,
and said, "Love and admiration from your fellow men
is all that anyone can ask."

Will's life was the American dream.

He was rich in friendship, fortune, and fame.

But he always loved people--all people--

with a grin on his face and a smile in his heart.

"I never met a man I didn't like."

ation Mourns Death of Favorite Son

ill Rogers ome Town rieves

leath of first citizen in
h Claremore, Oklahoma
, 16—(AP) —Will Rogers
etown, the Claremore that
lternately teased and
sed but always loved
ved tonight for it's first
zen.

oon after the word of the
norist's death was received
s were lowered to half-
st.

It can't be true. Nothing
rse could have happened,"
d his old friends who gath-
d in hushed groups to talk
Claremore's most famous
d beloved citizen.

here was no business in
aremore today.

Despite his absence of years
ill Rogers was still a Clar-
reite at heart. He main-
ned a residence here and the
wn's leading hotel is named
ter him. The airport bears his
me.

He sold the government the
nd for a new post office and
rned over the money, $4000,
the town for a new library.

"He told us it would have
better drawing power if we
named it Bill Murray or Clark
Gable," Said Harrison.

"Seeriously, though, he told
us it pleased him moreto see
his name in electric lights on
institution of service in his

Rogers had no fina
interest in the hotel.

But not only clarer
knew and loved Will
Rogers. The whole st
mourned.

The state will w
give them (Rogers